KU-478-096

THE ROYAL FAMILY
A pedigree showing the succession to the Throne from King George V to Queen Elizabeth II.

...nry [William ...derick Albert]. ...rn 31 March ...0. Created Duke ...Gloucester 1928. ...arried 6 Nov. ...35 Alice [Chris-...bel], daughter ...John [Montagu-...uglas-Scott], ...ke of Buccleuch ...d Queensberry

George [Edward Alexander Edmund]. Born 20 Dec. 1902. Created Duke of Kent 1934. Killed 25 August 1942. Married 29 Nov. 1934 Princess Marina, daughter of Nicholas, Prince of Greece and Denmark. Died 27 Aug. 1968.

John [Charles Francis] Born 12 July 1905. Died 18 Jany. 1919

[Victoria Alexandra Alice] Mary. Born 25 April 1897. Created The Princess Royal of Great Britain and Ireland 1931. Died 28 March 1965. Married 28 Feb. 1922 Henry [Lascelles], Viscount Lascelles, later Earl of Harewood. Died 24 May 1947.

Margaret [Rose] = Antony Armstrong-Jones. Born 21 Aug. 1930. Created Earl of Married 6 May Snowdon 1961. 1960.

Edward [Anthony Richard Louis]. Born 10 March 1964

Anne [Elizabeth Alice Louise]. Born 15 August 1950.

MACDONALD JUNIOR REFERENCE LIBRARY

HERALDRY

JRL 53

© B.P.C. Publishing Limited 1970
Second Impression 1974
ISBN 0 356 03238 8

MACDONALD JUNIOR REFERENCE LIBRARY

HERALDRY

MACDONALD EDUCATIONAL
49-50 POLAND STREET, LONDON W.1.

Editor's Note

This book provides an introduction to the subject of heraldry. It describes how heraldry developed and explains some of the terminology and laws pertaining to it. This volume deals mainly with heraldry in Britain but also mentions its use in other countries.

Acknowledgements

We gratefully acknowledge the assistance of Mr. J. P. Brooke-Little, *Richmond Herald,* in assembling material for this book.

Contents

How Heraldry Began ●

Heraldry began in Europe. It has always remained something specially European. Its uses have now spread to the Commonwealth and the New World, but it still has its roots in Europe. It is part of our European heritage.

The inspiration for heraldry came from the decoration of shields. Men had been decorating their shields since the time of the Ancient Greeks. It probably started with pieces of metal or leather being put on the shield to make it stronger. Then the pieces were arranged artistically, to form a pattern. Next, actual designs were placed on the shield. This improved the look of the shield and made it a more personal possession. Also, it made the shield-owner easy to recognise, even from a distance.

When armour came into use in Europe, warriors faced a new problem. Locked up in metal suits with closed visors, they all looked alike. The only way you could tell one man from another was by the design on his shield. So the shield *device* became very important. It was no longer just a decoration. It was a necessity.

In those early days the shield decoration was very simple. It stood out clearly and could be seen from a long way off. The same design was embroidered on the *surcoat* which was worn over armour. This garment was called a *coat of arms*.

The shield was therefore the beginning of heraldry. It has always been the most important part of it.

Thomas de Beauchamp, the Third Earl of Warwick, as he appears in the portrait on his seal. His arms are shown on his shield, his surcoat, and on the 'bard' or coat of his horse. His crest was the head and neck of a swan.

● How It Developed

Before long, his shield-picture became part of a man's possessions. When he died, his son inherited it, and then his grandson. It had become as important as a name. In some ways it identified him better. Many people could have the same name. A coat of arms belonged to one person alone.

In those early days heraldry was called 'armory'. It was the study of the decoration of arms. The Crusades did a lot to develop armory. The decorated shield, which protected a Crusader in battle, also told the world exactly who he was. Often, it even told whose son, grandson or nephew he was. This was useful, because Crusaders were of many different European nationalities. Often they did not understand each other's language, or the language of the land in which they were fighting. Most of them were unable to read or write. But they could all understand the shield-pictures, and so identify the owners. In those days, boys probably used to play at shield-spotting, just as they play at plane-spotting now.

During the years of the Crusades, the Crest, the Wreath and the Mantling were added to the shield of arms. By the time the Crusades were over, armory had become a special branch of learning. Shields themselves had become more complicated. Additional decorations had been put on to the first simple designs, perhaps in token of battle-honours. Great families had

Crusaders in battle surrounded by fierce Moslems. Each knight could be recognized easily by the device on his shield.

Knights jousting in the lists at a tournament.

intermarried, and their shield devices had been joined together in one bearing.

Then, in the twelfth century, the Herald came upon the scene. At first, he was merely an officer connected with tournaments. He had to call out the events and name the champions and their armorial bearings. So, of course, he had to be an expert on armory. It would never have done to make a mistake about a champion's arms. Family arms had become a matter of pride, and with good reason. They often told the history of a family.

Heralds became important people. They carried messages between kings and countries as well as presiding at courtly occasions. Wherever they went they were respected, and their persons were sacred in war. (That meant no one was allowed to attack them.) They wore splendid *tabards* embroidered with the arms of the king or country they served (see TABARD). They even had their own trumpeters to go before them and call silence for them by sounding a fanfare. Most important of all, they were responsible for all matters concerning armorial bearings. They made the laws and kept the records of arms.

So armory, the decoration of arms, became heraldry, the science of the Herald. A College of Heralds was formed. Those who were learning, and who assisted the Heralds, were called Pursuivants of Arms. (Pursuivant is pronounced purr-sweeve-ant.) The Heralds were Heralds of Arms. The most senior of them were Kings of Arms. At all times they were responsible for the heraldic matters of the country. So it is today.

11

● Heraldry Today

Heraldry is now part of our everyday existence. We seem to ignore it unless some great event of state occurs, something like a Coronation or an Investiture. Then, heraldic devices and flags blossom within the grey walls of our cities, and we buy souvenir items with heraldic decorations on them. But we live our lives surrounded by heraldry and don't realise it. You may have seen cars displaying a small plate bearing County arms. Many schools have a badge. The Forces certainly have theirs. Each town has its own coat of arms. Heraldic devices stare at us from park gates, town halls, public transport, churches and even pillar boxes.

Heraldry brings the best of our past into the world of today. The three golden lions in the Royal Arms first belonged to Richard Coeur-de-Lion (curr-de-lee-on) – Richard the Lionheart. Cadwallader's red dragon is still the badge of Wales. The White Horse of Kent was the device of the Anglo-Saxon Hengist-Horsa. The three seaxes (notched swords) in the arms of Middlesex and Essex are the weapons from which the East

The Investiture of the Prince of Wales at Caernarvon Castle.

The arms of the old City of Westminster include the emblems of Edward the Confessor and Henry VII who were responsible for the building of most of Westminster Abbey.

The grasshopper of the Gresham family and the Liver bird of the Bank of Liverpool were combined in the arms of Martins bank.

The arms of the Grocers' Company of London are used by Oundle, the school founded by the company.

The badge of the Royal Marines. The laurel wreath was won in 1761 for the storming of Belle Isle.

Saxons got their name. The Scottish Lion stands within a border of French fleurs-de-lis because of the ancient friendship between France and Scotland. There are three golden crowns and a ragged silver cross on the red shield of Colchester. The crowns recall the East Angles. The Cross is a memory of Saint Helena, who found the remains of Christ's Cross. Some say she was the daughter of King Cole.

The language and rules of heraldry are easy to learn. Almost every coat of arms has a story to tell. That is why heraldry is sometimes called 'the shorthand of history'.

Heraldry is for everyone who has something in which he takes pride. It might be his family. It might be his school, or his town, or his country, or his club. Republics and Communes, as well as Kingdoms, have their coats of arms. Guilds of workers have armorial bearings. The Grocers' Company of London since 1531 have had a shield 'Argent, a chevron gules between nine cloves sable'. These are also the arms used by Oundle school, which was founded by the Company.

Some day, the European nations may be made into an United States of Europe. In a way, heraldry has already done this. Its laws and traditions are European. It is already a part of the United States of Europe. It always has been.

13

● Heraldry A to Z

ACHIEVEMENT This is the official heraldic name for what is usually called a coat of arms. The actual coat of arms was the *surcoat* embroidered with armorial design. This was worn over armour. An Achievement is so called because it is a complete picture of all the heraldic decorations which have been achieved by one person. Here is how an Achievement may be made up.

Shield. There may be just a shield and nothing else. Without a shield there can be no Achievement.

In addition, it may have one, or more, or all of the following :

Crest. This started as a helmet decoration. There may be more than one Crest.

Helm. There may be more than one helm.

Mantling. The artistic drapes which sometimes surround a shield.

Torse or *Wreath.* The silken twist which holds the Mantling in place on the Helm (see TORSE).

Motto. This is sometimes taken from an old battle-cry.

Supporters. The two creatures sometimes found on either side of a shield, holding it up.

(See also the separate entries for SHIELD, CREST etc.)

An achievement of arms.

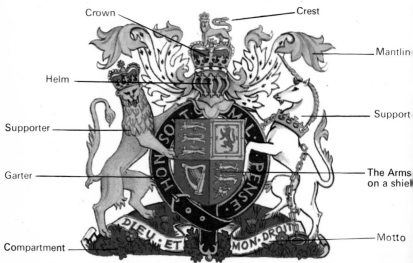

The Royal Arms.

The arms of the city of Liverpool refer to the mythical Liver bird.

A catherine wheel appears in the arms of St. Catherine's College, Cambridge.

The arms of Hertford are a Hart, and a ford represented by wavy blue lines.

ALLUSIVE ARMS, CANTING ARMS, AND ARMES PARLANTES

These are arms which refer to the name or trade of the bearer, or make a pun upon them. For instance, a pike appears in the arms of Pyke. Three martlets adorn the family arms of Martin. There are also canting mottoes (see MOTTOES).

ARMED

This term is used when referring to the teeth, talons, horns and claws of beasts, birds or monsters, especially when these are coloured differently from the rest of the creature. The following terms may be used to describe them:

Langued means 'tongued', so 'langued gules' means having a red tongue.

Attired is used to describe the antlers of stags and other beasts of the chase. The points of the antlers are called *tynes* and their number is usually stated. For example 'attired of ten tynes' means having antlers with ten points.

Beaked is the word used when referring to the beak of a bird or monster.

Unguled refers to the hoofs of a cloven-hoofed beast.

Disarmed is the word used if a creature is shown entirely without teeth, talons, horns or claws.

A lion rampant, armed and langued gules.

An Irish elk attired of twenty tynes.

A lion sejant erect affronté.

A swan ducally gorged and chained with wings displayed and inverted.

A
to

ATTITUDES The heraldic attitudes of beasts and monsters have special names. This simplifies the description of coats of arms. For instance a silver shield with a red lion rampant on it is described as: 'Argent, a lion rampant gules.' If the word *rampant* were not used one would have to say: 'Argent, a lion standing erect upon the left hind-leg. The other three paws are raised with the two fore-paws waving in the air. The head is held high and looking forward, the tail is erect. . . .' It would be very tiresome to enter into such a long description each time. Here, then, are the most important heraldic attitudes for beasts and monsters:

Addorsed. Back to back. Used for two animals so placed.

Affronté. Showing full front view to the observer.

At gaze. Used for stags shown standing sideways, with head facing the observer.

Combatant, or counter-rampant. Facing each other in combat.

Confronté. Facing one another.

Conjoined. Linked together.

Couchant. Lying down but not asleep.

Courant. Running.

Coward. With tail between legs.

Dormant. Lying down and asleep.

Lodged. The word used for the couchant position of stags.

Passant. Walking. Three paws on ground, right fore-paw raised in the air.

Passant guardant. As for passant, but with head turned to face the observer. The 'Lions of England' adopt this position.

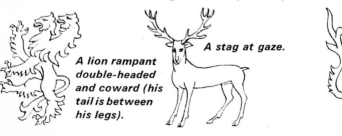

A lion rampant double-headed and coward (his tail is between his legs).

A stag at gaze.

Two

An eagle
collared
with wings
addorsed.

A stag springing.

nt guardant
er.

Passant reguardant. As for passant, but with head looking backwards.

Rampant. Described earlier in the first paragraph.

Rampant guardant. As for rampant, but with head turned to face the observer.

Rampant reguardant. As for rampant but with head looking backwards.

Salient. Springing. Hind-paws on ground, fore-paws in the air.

Segreant. Used for griffins only. The rampant position of the griffin.

Sejant. Seated, sideways to observer, looking in front.

Sejant erect. Seated with fore-paws raised.

Sejant erect affronté. As for sejant erect, but with the entire animal facing the observer. In the royal crest (not the shield) of Scotland, the lion is in this position.

Springing. A word used to describe deer and stags shown springing from the ground.

Statant. Standing with all four paws on ground.

Statant guardant. Standing with head turned to face the observer.

Statant reguardant. Standing and looking backwards.

Trippant. The passant position of a stag or other beast of the chase.

Vorant. In the act of devouring. The most famous example is the Viper Vorant of the Visconti family of Milan, where the serpent is shown eating a baby.

A viper
vorant.

A lion rampant
queue fourché
(with forked tail).

atant.

17

AUGMENTATIONS AND ABATEMENTS OF HONOUR

An *augmentation* is a mark of honour. It can be borne permanently upon a shield, where it provides a record of the noble deeds of ancestors. The family of Lane were granted a 'Canton of England' on their arms. This is a Canton charged with the three golden lions of England (see SUB-ORDINARIES). The Lane family still bear this augmentation though it was granted centuries ago by Charles II, because Jane Lane had helped him to escape from the Roundheads. More recently, Queen Victoria granted, to her faithful physician James Reid, the honourable augmentation of 'A lion rampant guardant or, on a chief gules.'

An *Abatement of Honour* is a mark of disgrace. It was placed on a shield to show that the bearer had been guilty of dishonourable behaviour. One kind of Abatement was the *Point* which cut off a corner of the shield. Another was the *Gore* by which a large part of the shield was blotted out. From this came the term 'a blot on the scutcheon'. Abatements were hardly ever used and could be removed if the knight did some good deed to atone for his crime.

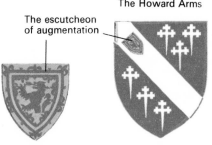

The Howard Arms

The escutcheon of augmentation

Thomas Howard, Second Duke of Norfolk, was awarded an augmentation by Henry VIII to commemorate his victory at Flodden. It took the form of the Royal Shield of Scotland, charged on the bend in the Howard arms (the shield having a demi-lion only, pierced through the mouth with an arrow).

BADGES AND KNOTS

Badges are often confused with Crests. Sometimes a crest is removed from a coat of arms and used as a badge, but this is quite wrong. The Crest always has a masculine or military connection but badges can be worn by women and children as well. (See CREST.) A badge may, but does not have to, repeat some feature of the crest or shield. The Plantagenet kings took their name from the *planta genista* (broom-flower) badge worn by their ancestor, Geoffrey of Anjou. But this never had a place in their coats of arms. The use of badges reached its height during the Wars of the Roses. The Yorkists took the white rose for their badge, while the Lancas-

18

trians had the red rose for theirs. Then the first Tudor king, Henry VII, united the two warring houses of Lancaster and York. He placed the white rose upon the red making the Tudor Rose.

There are two uses for badges. One is personal, as with the white ostrich feather badge and its motto 'Ich dien' (I serve) which is reserved for the Heir Apparent. The other use is more general, as when a badge is worn to demonstrate loyalty, or membership, or following. The White Hart badge of Richard II was not only famous in his time, but has been popular down the ages. It is still used as an inn-sign today. Children wear school badges on caps and blazers. In Scotland, the chief's crest-badge and motto may be worn by all his family, followers and clan. Popular national badges are the English Rose, the Scottish Thistle, the Irish Shamrock, the Welsh Leek, the Maple Leaf of Canada and the Kiwi of New Zealand.

The Armed Forces also have their badges. Each ship of the Royal Navy has its own, in which the device is surrounded by a rope and topped by a Naval Crown (see CROWN). Royal ships use a special badge-flag which we call the White Ensign. The Army wear regimental badges on caps, collars and buttons.

Finally, there is a small group of badges in which the design is in the form of twined cords or knots. One of the most interesting is the Lacy knot, a complicated knot which is a pun on the name of the Lacy family.

The badge of Harrow school.

The white rose of York.

The red rose of Lancaster.

The badge of the United Kingdom of Great Britain and Northern Ireland.

The Lacy knot.

The portcullis of the Beauforts and Tudors.

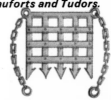

19

Preston

Oxford

Animals appear on the arms of everal English towns and cities.

Coventry

Warwick

BEASTS Beasts is a general term applied to the animals of heraldry. There are very many. Among the most popular are the lion, stag, horse, boar, bear, dog, wolf, fox, porcupine, badger and lizard. (For fabulous beasts, see MONSTERS.)

BIRDS Many different birds are found in heraldry. Among them are the eagle (see EAGLE), falcon, crow, owl, seagull, swan, chough, peacock, jackdaw, crane, pelican and swallow. One

A falcon belled and jessed.

which occurs frequently is the *martlet*, a swallow without any feet. The martlet is also the mark of cadency for a fourth son (see CADENCY). Here are some heraldic terms which refer to birds:

Belled and Jessed. This refers to falcons, and means that they are shown with bells attached to their feet by leather thongs called *jesses.*

A martlet.

A pelican in her piety.

Close. Standing on the ground with wings closed.

Combed and Jelopped. This term is applied to the fighting cock. It refers to the colour of its comb and wattles.

Displayed. With wings fully spread. The eagle often appears like this.

Rising. Standing with wings open, about to take off.

Volant. Shown in flight.

BLAZON To blazon a coat of arms means to describe it in correct heraldic terms. A blazon commences with a description of the shield, in the following order:

1. The field (background).
2. The principal charge or charges (see CHARGE).
3. Other charges (if any).
4. Minor charges (if any) lying upon major ones.
5. Marks of Cadency (see CADENCY).
6. Overall charge (if there is one).

After the shield, the Helm, Wreath, Crest, Mantling, and Motto are detailed. This is followed by a description of the Supporters if there are any. A blazon of a fairly simple shield might be as follows: *Azure, a stag's head erased attired of ten tynes or. On a chief argent a dolphin naiant vert. For difference a label of three points azure. Overall a bend ermine.*

BRASSES Heraldic brasses are metal memorial tablets found in old churches. Each is finely engraved with the likeness of some long-dead knight, lord or lady. They are sometimes life size and always of great interest. This is because they are a useful guide to the clothes, armour, heraldic bearings and insignia of the times in which they were made. There is a simple way of taking copies of heraldic brasses, known as brass-rubbing. This hobby is now enjoyed by people of all ages.

A brass-rubbing from the tomb of a knight.

CABOSHED Caboshed describes the head of an animal facing the observer and cut off so as to show no part of the neck. (See also ERASED and COUPED.)

CADENCY No two people may bear exactly the same coat of arms. Therefore, during the lifetime of their father, sons have to 'difference' the family arms with a mark of Cadency. In England there is a special mark for each son in order of birth. They may be of any colour, and are as follows:

First son	a label	Sixth son	a fleur-de-lis
Second son	a crescent	Seventh son	a rose
Third son	a mullet	Eighth son	a cross moline
Fourth son	a martlet	Ninth son	a double quatrefoil, or octofoil
Fifth son	an annulet		

The marks of difference for cadency.

These same marks are used in a set order to distinguish grandchildren and great-grandchildren. In Scotland there is a complicated system which makes use of coloured borders, varying lines and certain marks, used in a set order. This is also used for grandchildren and other descendants.

CHARGE A Charge is any object which appears upon the field of a shield. Charges may be human, animal, bird, fish, reptile, plant or tree. They may also be inanimate — that is, without life, like a spear or a ship. More than one charge may appear on a field, smaller charges may be placed on larger ones. It is rare to find a shield with no charge at all.

A shield checky vert and or.

CHECKY An all-over pattern of squares, rather like a chess-board, is called Checky. It is usually of two tinctures (colours). For example: 'Checky vert and or' means green and gold checks.

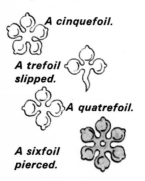

A cinquefoil.

A trefoil slipped.

A quatrefoil.

A sixfoil pierced.

CINQUEFOIL (or QUINTOFOIL), TREFOIL, QUATREFOIL, SIXFOIL AND OCTOFOIL (or DOUBLE QUATREFOIL) These are all flower-like forms with petals of equal and regular shape. The cinquefoil (sank-foil) has five petals, the trefoil three, the quatrefoil four, the sixfoil six and the octofoil eight. The octofoil is also the Mark of Cadency for a ninth son.

COUNTERCHANGING Counterchanging is an exchange of colour between a two-colour field and its charge. Imagine a shield divided vertically into two halves. One half is gold and the other is blue. Upon this gold-and-blue field a gold-and-blue rampant lion is placed. But the colours are reversed so that the blue half of the lion is on a gold field, and the gold half of the lion is on a blue field. This is heraldically described as: 'Party per pale or and azure, a lion rampant counterchanged'. The shield need not be divided by a vertical line as in the example given, but it can be divided in any of the ways described under PARTITIONS OF THE SHIELD. Other methods of counterchanging are sometimes seen, as in the arms of the old native Princes of North Wales.

Party per pale or and azure, a lion rampant counterchanged.

The shield of Llywelyn ap Gruffydd shows another form of counterchanging.

COUPED Couped means cut off cleanly. This term is used for the head or limb of an animal appearing as a charge. (For example: 'Purpure, a boar's head couped or.') (See also CABOSHED, ERASED.)

A boar's head couped at the back in the Scottish fashion.

CREST The term 'Crest' is misused more often than any other heraldic word. Sometimes the whole coat of arms is called a crest, quite wrongly. The crest is the small decoration which appears at the top of the coat of arms, above the helm. It probably began as a fan-shaped piece of metal which stuck up from the top of early helmets. Later, it came to be painted with a figure, and, later still, cut to the shape of a figure. Next, crests of leather or light wood were adopted. An early form of crest was an arrangement of feathers known as a *panache*. As the years passed crests became more and more fanciful, taking the form of animals or birds, or inanimate objects of many kinds. When men no longer

A panache of feathers is the crest of John, Lord Scrope.

The crest, chapeau and helm of the Black Prince's achievement.

The Garter Stall Plate of Sir Lewis Robessart shows his large and curious crest. It is the head of a Turkish sultan wearing both a cap and crown, with a catherine wheel on top.

The arms of Sir Winston Spencer Churchill include the arms of Spencer quartered with those of Churchill. There are two helms and two crests.

wore armour, the crest which used to stand above the helmet was transferred to the painted coat of arms. There is greater variety to be found in crest designs than in the designs of shields. An Achievement may have more than one crest. If a Royal Licence is granted it may have two, or three. With the exception of the Sovereign, no female may inherit a crest. She may inherit her father's shield design, which she will bear upon a lozenge (see WOMEN'S ARMS). Crests usually stand upon the Torse (see TORSE). But some ancient families bear their crests upon crest-coronets. Others use *chapeaux* (red velvet caps lined with ermine). Others still, with old naval traditions, use naval crowns (see CROWN).

CRINED Crined is a term used to describe the hair or mane of a charge. For example 'a unicorn rampant argent, armed, crined and unguled or' (a white unicorn rampant, with horn, mane and hoofs of gold).

CROSS The cross is one of the honourable Ordinaries. (See ORDIN-ARIES.) When used as an Ordinary it can be varied by using one or other of the decorative Lines of Partition. (See PARTITIONS OF THE SHIELD.) The Cross raguly in the arms of Colchester has already been mentioned. The Cross is also used as a charge, and there are nearly four hundred different kinds of cross used in heraldry. Among them are the Calvary Cross, the Cross couped, the Cross botonny, the Cross potent, the Cross formy, the Patriarchal Cross, the Tau. Cross and the Maltese Cross. Another popular form is the Cross-crosslet, in which each arm is crossed again. One often finds the background of the shield scattered with Cross-crosslets. In this case the field is said to be *crusily*. (See FIELD.) A blue shield scattered with gold Cross-crosslets would be 'Azure, crusilly or'.

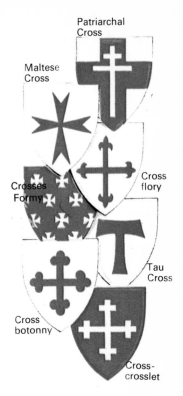

Some heraldic crosses.

CROWN Many different Crowns are used in heraldry. A beautiful one is the Astral Crown, in which the circlet is surmounted by four stars, each star held within outspread wings. Another is the Naval Crown, decorated alternately with the stems and sails of ships. This Crown is used for ships' badges of the Royal Navy, and also for the arms of many towns which have naval associations, such as Plymouth. The Mural Crown used in civic heraldry resembles a brick wall. Others are the Eastern, the Open, the Palisado and the Celestial Crowns.

The Mural Crown which is used in civic heraldry.

The Naval Crown.

The Astral Crown.

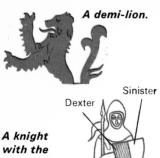

A demi-lion.

DEMI- Demi- means half. It is a word much used in heraldry where half a beast, bird or monster is often used as a charge or crest. The demi-lion is especially popular. Usually, the upper, or front half, is the part shown.

Sinister

Dexter

A knight with the dexter side of his shield shaded.

DEXTER This means right-hand side. The Dexter side of the shield is always the right-hand side from the point of view of the person standing behind it. Looking at the front of the shield or a picture of it, the Dexter side is on the left. (See also SINISTER.)

DIFFERENCING Coats of arms are differenced in order to distinguish the different branches of a family. In mediaeval times this was done by adding charges, especially a bordure, or by changing the colour of the field or charges. Today, small charges are added to the shield. (See CADENCY.)

The arms of Sandwich, which is one of the Cinque Ports, show lions dimidiating ships.

DIMIDIATED Dimidiation was the earliest method of joining together the shields of husband and wife. Each shield was cut in half vertically, and the left half of one shield was then joined to the right half of the other. This often resulted in two utterly different things being joined together in the middle. For instance half a lion might be joined to half a ship.

EAGLE The Eagle is such an important bird in heraldry that it deserves a heading to itself. The Romans used the Eagle as the proud standard of an army legion. The Emperor Charlemagne also took it for his device. More recently, the double-headed eagle was used by the Austro-Hungarian Empire. Napoleon took the eagle for his device, and the modern Americans also use it. It appears more often and in more varied forms than any other bird. As well as appearing *double-headed, rising, displayed,*

26

The arms of the British Broadcasting Corporation have two eagles with bugle-horns as supporters. They are emblems of proclamation.

The American eagle is shown displayed proper, grasping an olive branch and a bundle of arrows, with the shield of the United States placed on its breast.

volant, close and preying, it is sometimes found without a beak, legs or claws. In this form it is called an *Alerion*. Often, an eagle's head, or leg, or wing is used as a charge. When more than one eagle appears on a shield they are sometimes called *Eaglets*, as in the arms of Piers Gaveston: 'vert, six eaglets or' (six gold eagles on a green field).

The six birds in the arms of Gaveston are called Eaglets.

EMBLAZON To 'emblazon' a coat of arms is to paint it in its correct colours as described in the blazon. (See BLAZON.)

ERASED Erased means torn off so as to leave ragged edges. This is often done with the head or leg of an animal used as a charge or crest. (See also CABOSHED and COUPED.)

ESCUTCHEON An escutcheon is a shield, especially one used as a charge in a coat of arms. (See also INESCUTCHEON.)

FIELD The field is the background of a shield, upon which charges are placed (see CHARGE). It can consist of a colour, a fur, or a metal (see TINCTURES, FURS). It can be divided so that it is of more than one colour. (See PARTITIONS OF THE SHIELD.) It can be scattered with small objects, when it is said to be *semé* (see SEMÉ). It is the thing which is mentioned first in a

27

description of a shield of arms. It is not necessary to say, 'on a field argent, a lion rampant gules'. It is enough to say: 'Argent, a lion rampant gules'. It is understood that the field is the first thing to be mentioned in a blazon.

FIMBRIATED Fimbriated means 'edged with'. 'A cross vert fimbriated or' means a green cross edged with gold.

FISH These are popular in heraldry, and fish of many different kinds are found on shields and crests. The heraldic term 'fish' also includes whales, dolphins, crabs, lobsters, and fish shells. The dolphin is the most important heraldic fish and is often used.

A dolphin embowed.

An escallop

Argent a cross potent fitchy gules.

It was the royal sign of the Dauphins of France. Fish have their own heraldic attitudes. Here are some of them:

Embowed. Curved like a bow.

Hauriant. Upright, as if standing on its own tail.

Naiant. Swimming along horizontally.

Uriant. Head downwards, placed vertically, as if diving.

FITCHED, FITCHEE or FITCHY When the base of a Cross is shown pointed at the foot like a dagger, it is called fitchée.

FLAGS There are three kinds of flag used in heraldry.

Banner. This is a square or oblong flag showing the personal arms of the bearer. The Royal Banner is flown over any building in which the Sovereign is present. It is often wrongly called the Royal Standard. The Flags of Arms which are hung over the stalls of the Knights of the Garter in St. George's Chapel, Windsor, are banners.

Pennon. This is a small narrow flag, pointed or swallow-tailed at the end. It is the personal ensign of the bearer and often carries his badge or some other device. Sometimes it is fringed with gold. In ancient times, if a knight had distinguished himself in battle, the King would tear the tail off his pennon, while still on the battlefield. The knight's pennon was thereby made into a banner, and the knight was advanced to the rank of *banneret.*

Standard. This is a ceremonial flag used for pageantry. It was much used at jousts and tournaments. The standard is long and narrow, pointed or swallow-tailed at the end, and richly fringed. The more important the person, the longer his Standard. The Standard displays badges and livery colours. Mottoes are placed bendwise (slanted) across them.

The Standard of Sir Henry de Stafford.

FLEUR-DE-LIS A formal flower-design. It is usually taken to represent the lily, though its shape is more like that of the iris. It is one of the most popular charges. Sometimes it is the only charge on the field. Sometimes it appears in groups. It is often used to decorate Ordinaries or Sub-Ordinaries. (See ORDINARIES and SUB-ORDINARIES.) The arms of the City of Wakefield show a gold fleur-de-lis fimbriated (edged with) ermine. A rather unusual form is when it appears *jessant* (shooting forth) from the face of a leopard or lion. It is also the Mark of Cadency for a sixth son. (See CADENCY.) When the field is *semé* (scattered with) fleurs-de-lis it is said to be *semé-de-lis.* A bordure decorated with them is called a *bordure flory.*

A double tressure flory counterflory surrounding a leopard's face jessant-de-lis.

More than anything else the fleur-de-lis is associated with the arms of France. The early French arms consisted of a blue shield scattered with several gold fleurs-de-lis and was termed 'Azure, semé-de-lis or'. This coat is now called France Ancient. Charles V of France reduced the number of fleurs-de-lis to three. This is called France Modern. In 1340, when

The old arms of France, called France Ancient, were 'Azure, semé-de-lis or'.

Edward III of England claimed the French throne, he quartered the Lilies of France with the Lions of England in his Royal Arms. The Royal Arms of England were then described as 'Quarterly France and England'. The French quartering remained in the Royal Arms until 1801, when it was removed. But there are still fleurs-de-lis in the arms of the United Kingdom. They decorate the 'double tressure flory-counter-flory', which surrounds the Scottish lion.

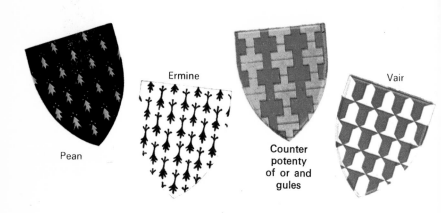

Pean

Ermine

Counter
potenty
of or and
gules

Vair

Some of the forms in which furs are used in heraldry.

FURS There are two main furs used in heraldry, *Vair* and *Ermine*. Each has a number of different forms.

Vair is always azure and argent – that is, blue and white. The name is based on the fur made from the skin of a small squirrel called *Ver* or *Vair*. It was blue-grey on top and white underneath. When a number of skins were sewn together the result was a pattern of bell-shaped figures alternately blue and white. Cinderella really wore slippers of *Vair* (fur) and not *verre* (glass)

Here are some different kinds of Vair.

Beffroi (belfry) or *Gros-Vair*. Large Vair.

Menu-vair (miniver). Small Vair.

Counter-vair, vair-en-pale, vair-en-pointe. Different arrangements of the segments.

Potent (old word for crutch). In this the segments are shaped like the top of a crutch. Also *counter-potent.*

Vair Ancien. This is an early form of Vair. It was used without a charge in the shield of the de Ferrers family. This can be seen in the stained glass windows of Dorchester Church, in Oxfordshire.

Vairy or Potenty. This is a field patterned as for Vair or Potent but in tinctures other than blue and white. For example, 'Vairy of or and gules' (gold and red) and 'Potenty of or and gules'.

Ermine is a white fur with black ermine-tails on it. This fur also has some different forms.

Ermines. Black fur with white tails.

Erminois. Gold fur with black tails.

Pean. Black fur with gold tails.

Erminites (rare). White fur with black tails and red spots.

In Ermine we have another example of an ancient shield with no charge upon its field. This is the shield of Brittany, which is simply 'Ermine.'

GARTER The Order of the Garter is one of the oldest and most honoured Orders of Chivalry. It was started by Edward III. The story is that one day, when Princess Joan of Kent was dancing at a Court Ball in Calais, her garter fell to the ground. In those strict days this was considered very shameful. But King Edward picked it up and bound it round his own leg, reproving the mocking courtiers with the words : 'Honi soit qui mal y pense' (Evil be to him who evil thinks). Ever since then these words have been

The insignia of the Order of the Garter.

The Garter

The Star

the motto of the Order of the Garter. Princess Joan was known as The Fair Maid of Kent. She later married the Black Prince, son of Edward III. The Black Prince was one of the first Knights of the Garter. Since that time the Heir Apparent has always been one of the Garter Knights. The Garter is taken to be a sign of the unity by which all the Knights are bound together in companionship.

GENEALOGY The science of tracing one's descent from ancestors is called genealogy. It plays an important part in heraldry because arms are inherited.

The badge of Richard II, a white hart gorged with a royal diadem or and chained.

GORGED Gorged is the term which is used when any figure is shown with a collar round its neck. Very often the collar is in the form of a crown. The White Hart of Richard II is 'gorged with a royal diadem or' (collared with a gold crown).

GOUTTE OR DROP The goutte is a drop of liquid. If the field is scattered with drops it is said to be *goutté*. A field scattered with gold drops is *goutté d'or*. But the other colours, argent, azure, vert and so on, are blazoned in a special way.

Goutté d'eau (water) for drops of argent (silver).
Goutté de larmes (tears) for drops of azure (blue).
Goutté de sang (blood) for drops of gules (red).
Goutté d'huile (oil) for drops of vert (green).
Goutté de poix (dried peas) for drops of sable (black).

A field 'goutté de poix' is shown on the arms of the city of Chichester.

This is a ruling which only applies to English heraldry. Continental heraldry makes use of the ordinary terms such as *goutté d'argent*.

The goutte sometimes appears as a charge in its own right as in the arms of Harbottle: 'Azure, three gouttes in bend or' (three gold drops in a diagonal line on a blue shield).

GRANT OF ARMS To be given a Grant of Arms is to be given official permission to bear arms. In England this is given by the Crown, through the King of Arms, and in Scotland by the Lyon Court. (See LYON.)

The Grant of Arms to the Drapers' Company of London, 1439.

Or

Argent

HATCHING Hatching is a method whereby heraldic colours and metals can be shown in black and white (see TINCTURES). This is useful because colouring is not always possible in printed books. Hatching is done by using lines and dots on a white background, as shown below:

Azure

Or (gold) dots on white background
Argent (silver) plain white
Gules (red) vertical lines
Azure (blue) horizontal lines
Vert (green) lines in bend (slanted lines from dexter chief (or top) to sinister base)
Purpure (purple) lines in bend-sinister (slanted lines from sinister chief to dexter base)
Sable (black) vertical and horizontal lines crossing to form small squares

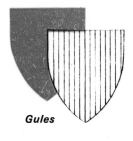

Gules

Sable

Purpure

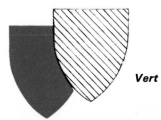

Vert

Murrey, tenné and sanguine are three other tinctures that can also be indicated by hatching.

This Funeral Hatchment indicates that the wife who bore these arms is dead. While her husband is still alive the background on the dexter side of the hatchment remains white.

HATCHMENTS (These must not be confused with HATCHING, above.) Hatchments should be called Funeral Hatchments. They were used only after a person was dead. On the death of an armigerous person, his or her armorial bearings were painted on a black lozenge-shaped panel. This was placed on the front of his house as a sign of mourning. It was kept there for about a year and then removed to the local church, where it would stand permanently. Hatchments carried the full armorial bearing of the dead person except for the motto, which was generally removed and replaced by some phrase such as 'Requiescat in pace' (May he rest in peace) or 'Resurgam' (I will rise again).

HELM OR HELMET In an Achievement the Helm is shown on top of the shield. The crest is placed on a *torse* above it (see TORSE). For peers, the helm stands on top of each man's particular kind of coronet. The type and position of the helm show the rank of the bearer of the arms, so no one can pretend to be more important than he is.

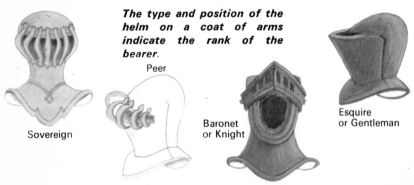

The type and position of the helm on a coat of arms indicate the rank of the bearer.

Peer

Sovereign

Baronet or Knight

Esquire or Gentleman

Royalty. An all-gold helmet facing forwards. The open front has bars guarding it.

Peers. A silver helm with gold bars over the open grille. The helmet is placed sideways, with its front to the dexter side of the shield (see DEXTER).

Baronets and Knights. Steel helmet, facing forward with open visor.

Esquires and Gentlemen. Steel helmet with closed visor placed sideways, with its front to the dexter side of the shield.

Two nags' heads erased appear as charges on the arms of Samuel Pepys the diarist.

The county arms of Kent show a white horse rampant.

A horse, ducally gorged, is the dexter supporter on the arms of the Earl of Ellesmere.

HORSE The horse played an important part in the development of chivalry. Such words as chivalry and cavalier come from the French word for horse, *cheval.* In ancient times the horse was a symbol of power and prestige. The early Saxons used it as their symbol, and the great White Horse carved out of the chalk on the downs of Berkshire still reminds us of the victory of King Alfred over the Danes in 871. Horses are used as charges, crests or supporters. Two famous heraldic horses are the White Horse of Kent, which is always shown rampant, and the White Horse of Hanover, which is shown courant.

IMPALE To impale is to join together two shields such as those of a husband and wife. The complete shield design of each is displayed on one half of the impaled shield. This is a better practice than the earlier one of dimidiating (see DIMIDIATED).

Effigies of John Eyer and his wife Margaret appear with their arms on their tomb in Narburgh Church in Norfolk. She was one of the daughters of Sir Thomas Blenhailet but she was not his heraldic heiress.

The arms of John Eyer Esquire

The arms of Margaret Eyer. The arms of her husband are impaled with those of her father.

If a wife's shield is impaled with that of her husband, it means that the wife is not an heraldic heiress. She cannot inherit her father's arms because she has brothers who will do so. She may impale them with her husband's during her lifetime only, and her children cannot inherit them after her death (see also INESCUTCHEON).

INESCUTCHEON An inescutcheon is a small shield, bearing its own charges, which is placed in the centre of a large shield. A special form of inescutcheon is the *Escutcheon of Pretence.* When a woman who is an

Left: the arms of the Prince of Wales bear an inescutcheon ensigned with a coronet.

heraldic heiress marries, her husband will carry her arms in a small shield set in the very middle of his. This is called an *Escutcheon of Pretence*, because the man only pretends to them during his wife's lifetime. When he and his wife are both dead, the children will inherit both their sets of arms and will quarter them together in their own shields (see also QUARTER).

INVERTED

Inverted means upside down. This term is used to describe the wings of birds when they are shown with their tips pointing downwards.

Right: a dove, wings addorsed and inverted.

LEOPARDS OF ENGLAND

This term gives rise to a lot of confusion, because the *Leopards of England* are in fact lions. The confusion arose in this way. The lion has always been regarded as the most noble of all the heraldic beasts. In the early days of heraldry he was thought to be so very noble that he ought to be shown only in the most noble position of all – *rampant.* Some French heralds went even further. They insisted that a lion shown in any other position was not to be called a lion. So the three golden lions *passant guardant* of England came to be called leopards because they were not in the rampant position. However, in the end common sense won. For many centuries now this fussy mediaeval custom has been dropped and the Lions of England are called lions.

The Leopards of England appear in the first and fourth quarters of the Royal Arms on the Royal Banner. They are really three golden lions passant guardant.

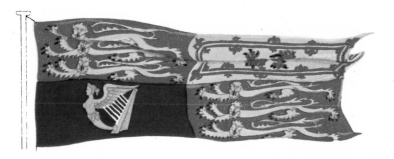

An heraldic lion rampant.

The Lions of England.

LION The Lion is the most noble beast of all. He is seen more often, and in more attitudes, than any other beast. He appears in whole or in part. Sometimes he is dimidiated with unlikely objects such as ships or fish (see DIMIDIATED). Sometimes he is beheaded. Sometimes he has two heads, or two tails, or three bodies. He is seen wounded, or with fangs dripping blood, or with his limbs severed, which is called 'coupled in all his joints'. He appears as supporter, charge or crest. Wherever and whenever he appears, he is an important figure. In England, Scotland and Wales, he is the most important feature of the Royal Arms.

The Lions of England are the three golden lions *passant guardant* which were first borne as a coat of arms by Richard Lionheart. They have appeared in the Royal Arms of Great Britain ever since his time. They had the shield to themselves through the reigns of King John, Henry III, Edward I and Edward II. But when Edward III became King, he claimed the French throne as well, through his mother Isabella of France. The fleurs-de-lis

Left: the Lion of England, one of the Queen's Beasts.

A lion rampant reguardant.

A lion dormant.

which he quartered with the Lions of England were only dropped from the arms in 1801. To-day, the Lions of England occupy the first and fourth quarters of the arms. The Lion of Scotland occupies the second quarter and the Irish harp the third. The golden lion *passant guardant* is now regarded as the royal Lion of England. The *Canton of England* which is sometimes granted as an Augmentation of Honour is : a canton gules with three lions passant guardant in pale or.

The Lion of Scotland is a noble animal with a fierce red colour, and blue claws and tongue. The Royal Arms of Scotland are : or, a lion rampant gules, armed and langued azure, within a double tressure flory-counter-flory gules.

The Lions of Wales. The old Princes of North Wales bore four red and gold lions counterchanged (see COUNTER-CHANGING). The Princes of Deheubarth (South West Wales) bore a gold lion rampant.

Lioncels. In ancient heraldry, when more than one lion appeared on a shield, they were called *lioncels*.

A lion's head erased.

A lion's paw couped.

A lion's jambe (leg) erased.

The crest of the Earl of Ellesmere is a lion rampant.

The lion of Hesse-Darmstadt is double-tailed and crowned.

This lion is being used as a supporter but he is in an unusual unheraldic. position.

LIVERY COLOURS The colours in which servants, retainers or soldiers of a great lord or king were dressed were called Livery Colours. They are supposed to be made up of the chief metal and the chief colour on the shield, like the mantling and torse. This is not always so. The Plantagenet livery colours were scarlet and white. During the Wars of the Roses Lancastrians used blue and white while Yorkists had blue and murrey. When the Tudors came to the throne they adopted white and green. The Stuarts used gold and scarlet: gold for the Lions of England, scarlet for the background of the shield. Gold and scarlet are still the livery colours of the United Kingdom.

The official coat of Lord Lyon King of Arms.

LYON The Lord Lyon King of Arms is the Chief Officer of Arms in Scotland. His heraldic office is the oldest in Great Britain. In Scotland the control of heraldry is protected by the law. Therefore Lord Lyon has very great powers. He is a great officer of state and holds his authority from the Crown. It is high treason to strike him or to hinder him in the exercise of his authority. He deals with all matters regarding the use of heraldry in Scotland and his powers include those of fine and imprisonment.

Originally, the mantling, or lambrequin, was a piece of material that kept the sun off the helm.

MANTLING OR LAMBREQUIN The Mantling or Lambrequin is the name given to the folds of material which fall from the Helm and float around the shield. The name is taken from the mantlet, or short cape, worn by Crusaders. This was fixed to the helmet by a twist of material or cord. It hung down as far as the shoulders and kept the hot sun off the metal armour and helmet. It also helped to tangle sword-blows aimed at the neck.

In combat, mantlets often got very hacked-about and tattered. These tatters were regarded as proof of courage and were copied in the coats of arms. Over the years, the painted mantlings in armorial bearings became very fanciful. The outside was of the most important colour, and the doubling or reverse was the colour of the most important metal. Now any colour or metal may be used. The Royal mantling is gold lined with ermine.

Tattered mantling showed that the wearer had taken part in fierce battles so it was copied in the coat of arms. This has led to the leafy, waving fronds that now often appear. In very special circumstances a badge may be borne on the mantling. This occurs in the arms of the Heraldry Society which are shown on the cover of this book.

MARSHALLING OF ARMS By the end of the 13th century heraldic arms were no longer just a means of recognition. They could also be used to tell the world that their bearer had made an important marriage, or that he claimed to be lord of more than one domain, or that he held some high office. This was done by using two or more sets of arms grouped together in one bearing. This combining of coats of arms is called the Marshalling of Arms. An early form of marshalling was the Compounding of Arms. This means charges were taken from two or more separate shields and used together to form a new and different shield. Other methods of marshalling are Dimidiation, Impalement and Quartering. (See DIMIDIATED, IMPALE, QUARTER.)

MATRICULATION OF ARMS The official recording of arms in the lists of the College of Heralds is called the Matriculation of Arms. No arms are legal unless they have been so registered.

The Red Dragon of Wales.

The Unicorn of Edward III.

The Black Dragon of Ulster.

MONSTERS In heraldry, a monster is any beast which is not a known species of animal. The term 'monster' does not necessarily mean that it is evil or wicked. Monsters really deserve a book to themselves, as they are very curious and fascinating. The following are the most important:

Unicorn. This is the purest and most romantic of the monsters, though he is also brave and fierce. The Scottish Unicorn is one of the Supporters of the Royal Arms.

Dragon. This was probably the fiercest of them all. A red dragon is the royal badge of Wales.

Griffin. The Griffin is a special favourite with a long history going back to ancient Crete. He is half-lion and half-eagle, and therefore a very noble character.

Heraldic Panther. This has nothing to do with the real panther. He is one of the most remarkable of the heraldic monsters. He is wholly virtuous, good,

A Panther gorged with a palisado crown

The Beaufort Yale.

The Heraldic Antelope or Ibex.

A Salamander.

A Phoenix

gentle and pure. His breath is so sweet-smelling that it enchants all who come near. He is always shown *flammant.* That is, with flames coming from mouth and nostrils. But these flames are really an attempt to illustrate his perfumed breath.

Cockatrice. This is the only utterly wicked heraldic monster. He is a revolting creature, only about a foot in length. He has the head and feet of a cock, with body and wings like those of the dragon, plus a barbed poisoned tail. He is treacherous and murderous. His breath and his glance can both kill. Only the *basilisk* can fight and overcome him. This is a cockatrice with a dragon-like head on his tail.

Among the many other monsters of heraldry are the following : *Amphiptere, Amphisboena, Bagwyn, Camelopard, Centaur, Enfield, Harpy, Mermaid, Pegasus, Phoenix, Salamander, Satyr, Sphinx, Wyvern* and *Yale.*

A Wyvern.

A Mermaid.

The Heraldic Sea-Lion.

A Cockatrice, the most wicked heraldic monster.

43

MOTTOES Mottoes are less important in English heraldry than in Scottish. In England the motto is not considered an essential part of the Achievement. It is rarely included in the Grant of Arms. It is not hereditary. No permission is needed to have one. It can be changed as often as wished, and is normally placed on a scroll under the shield. In Scotland the motto is part of the Grant of Arms, which specifies where it is to be placed. It cannot be changed without a re-matriculation of the new motto (see MATRICULATION OF ARMS). The blazon must state where the motto is to be placed. In Ireland there seems to be no set rule.

Mottoes are generally in Latin or in French. These were the languages used by clergy and the Normans in Mediaeval days. There are, however, mottoes in English, Gaelic, Welsh, Erse and Greek.

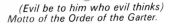

(Evil be to him who evil thinks)
Motto of the Order of the Garter.

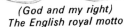

(God and my right)
The English royal motto

(Through difficulty to the stars)
The Royal Air Force Motto.

The Scout motto.

(The red dragon gives the lead)
The Welsh badge motto.

Mottoes are supposed to have started in the distant past as battle-cries. This can only apply to a few of them. The English royal motto 'Dieu et mon droit' (God and my right) was almost certainly an old battle-cry. But the splendid Scottish royal motto 'Nemo me impune lacessit' (no one provokes me with impunity) is rather too long to have been a battle-cry. It might well have been a *sword-rune.*

(A strong shield is the leader's safeguard)
The Fortescue motto.

;word-runes were sayings which
vere engraved on swords. Some of
hem were later adopted as mottoes.
\part from national mottoes there are
lso Army, Navy and Air Force mottoes.
;ome heraldic mottoes make a pun
n the shield, crest or badge device.
)thers are a play upon the names or
he badge device, or a play upon the
ames of the holders.

(Well done)
The Weldon motto.

(Form no mean wish)
The Neville motto.

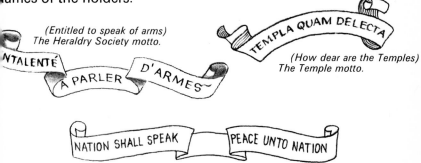

(Entitled to speak of arms)
The Heraldry Society motto.

(How dear are the Temples)
The Temple motto.

Motto of the British Broadcasting Corporation.

Some mottoes refer to family exploits or past family history.
)ne of the saddest of these is 'Fuimus' (we have been). It was
he motto of the Bruce family, who were Kings of Scotland in
he past. The motto of the Redclyffe family, 'Caen, Cressy,
:alais', calls to mind the honours gained by their ancestor Sir
lohn Redclyffe in those battles. In the same way, 'Agincourt',
he motto of the Walker family, recalls ancient battle-honours.
:inally, here is a curious motto which belonged to the family of
Vlartin. It says: 'He who looks at Martin's ape, Martin's ape
hall look at him.'

NOWED Nowed means twisted or knotted. It describes serpents
hown in twisted form. The lion sometimes appears with his
ail nowed.

Chevronels

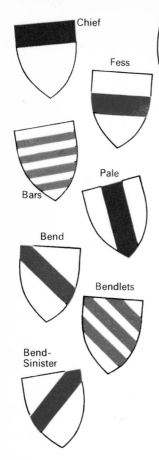

The Honourable Ordinaries.

ORDINARIES The Ordinaries are sometimes called the Honourable Ordinaries. They are an important group of charges (see CHARGE). They are made up of simple bands and regular figures. They appear over and over again in coats of arms. Often they have other charges placed on them. Here is a description of each of them.

Chief. A broad band across the top of the shield.

Fess. A broad horizontal band in the middle of the shield.

Bar. A smaller version of the Fess. It is seldom used singly.

Pale. A broad vertical band down the middle of the shield.

Bend. A broad band slanted across the shield from dexter chief (top) to sinister base (see DEXTER and SINISTER).

Bendlet. A narrower version of the Bend. It is seldom used singly.

Bend-Sinister and *Bendlet-Sinister.* This is the same as Bend and Bendlet, but placed the other way round.

Chevron. This is a broad, upside-down V placed in the centre of the shield, not quite reaching either to the top or the bottom. The name comes from the French word 'chevron' meaning a rafter. In the British Army it is worn reversed as a badge on the sleeve, when it denotes the rank of corporal or sergeant.

Chevronel. This is a smaller version of the chevron. It rarely appears singly.

Cross. A broad cross set in the centre of the shield, its ends touching the outside. However, its ends can be cut short and it has many different forms (see CROSS).

Pall   Shakefork   Saltire   Cross

Pile. A triangular wedge which has its wide part at the top of the shield, and its point not quite reaching the bottom.

Pall. A figure like the letter Y, with all its ends touching the edges of the shield.

Shakefork (or *Pairle*). A pall with its limbs cut short so that they don't reach the edges of the shield.

Saltire. A figure like a broad X, its ends touching the outsides of the shield. It is popular in Scotland as it is the Cross of St. Andrew, the Patron Saint.

PARTITIONS OF THE SHIELD The field of a shield may be divided in a number of special ways. It is then called a *party field* or a *parted field.* As these divisions are like the Ordinaries they are given the same names (see ORDINARIES).

Party per fess. Divided by a horizontal line in the middle.

Party per pale. Divided by a vertical line in the middle.

Party per bend. Divided by a slanting line from dexter top to sinister base.

Party per bend-sinister. A slanting line as for *per bend,* but in the opposite direction.

Party per chevron. Divided by a chevron in the middle.

Party per cross or *quarterly.* Divided by a cross into four quarters.

Party per saltire. Divided by a saltire into four quarters.

In some cases, namely fess, bend, pale and chevron, the lines may be repeated all over the field. It is then said to be *barry, bendy, paly* or

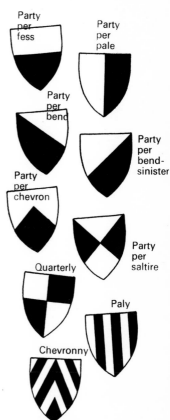

The ways in which the shield may be divided.

Party per fess

Party per pale

Party per bend

Party per bend-sinister

Party per chevron

Quarterly

Party per saltire

Paly

Chevronny

47

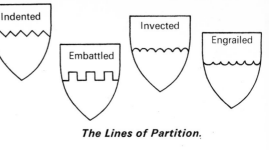

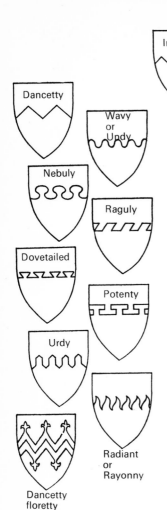

The Lines of Partition.

chevronny, usually of two tinctures.

The dividing of the field of a shield may be done with decorative *Lines of Partition*, instead of straight ones. Once again, there are a set number of these, each with its own heraldic name.

As with the straight Lines of Partition, the decorative lines can be repeated all over the shield, making fields of *barry-wavy*, *paly-wavy*, *bendy-wavy*, *barry-potenty*, *bendy-embattled*, *chevronny-nebuly* and so on. 'Barry-wavy argent and azure' is generally taken to represent water.

The Ordinaries can also be done in these decorative lines, so that you have a *bend engrailed*, or a *chevron-embattled*, or a *fess-dancetty*, and so on.

PROPER Proper means 'shown in its natural colours' and not in heraldic tinctures (see TINCTURES). A charge which is proper may lie upon furs, metals or colours.

QUARTER To quarter a shield is to place more than one coat of arms upon it. The shield is divided into quarters horizontally and vertically, and one coat is placed in each quarter. If a son inherits arms from both parents, he will quarter both coats in his own shield (see INESCUTCHEON). Usually, when two coats of arms are being quartered, the more important one is placed in the first and fourth quarters. The less important goes into the second and third quarters. A shield may be 'quartered' many times. A quarter itself may be quartered again. But many quarterings do not necessarily add to the honour or importance of a shield. Moreover, a much-quartered shield is often not very pleasing to the eye, and certainly looks very confused. For this reason many people do not make use of all the quarterings to which they are entitled. A very high number of quarterings is recorded for a family in Yorkshire, whose blazon begins: 'Quarterly of three hundred and fifty six . . .' and runs into several pages of description.

QUEEN'S BEASTS When the young Queen Elizabeth II was crowned, ten splendid heraldic beasts were made, which graced the Annexe of Westminster Abbey. They were all noble and honourable beasts inherited by the Queen from her ancestors. They were taken from the shields and badges of past Kings, Queens, Princes and heroes. They were: the golden *Lion of England,* the golden *Griffin of Edward III,* the silver *Falcon of the Plantagenets,* the black *Bull of Clarence,* the white *Lion of Mortimer,* the silver *Yale of Beaufort,* the white *Greyhound of Richmond,* the red *Dragon of Wales,* the white *Unicorn of Scotland,* the white *Horse of Hanover.*

The Falcon of the Plantagenets.

The white Greyhound of Richmond.

The white Lion of Mortimer.

The black Bull of Clarence.

The Griffin of Edward III

49

A Rose, budded, slipped and leaved.

ROSE The heraldic rose is a simple flower figure always shown with five petals. It has a *barb* between each petal and a seed, or five seeds, in the centre. If it is shown with a stem it is said to be *slipped*. The Rose of Lancaster is red. The Rose of York is white. The Tudor Rose is a white rose on a red one (see BADGES AND KNOTS).

ROUNDEL The Roundel is one of the Sub-Ordinaries. It is a circular object differently named according to its colour.

Bezant. A roundel or (gold).

Plate. A roundel argent (silver).

Torteau. A roundel gules (scarlet).

Hurt. A roundel azure (blue).

Ogress, Pellet, Gunstone. A roundel sable (black).

Pomme. A roundel vert (green).

Orange. A roundel tenné (tawny).

Golpe. A roundel purpure (purple).

Guze. A roundel sanguine (deep crimson).

Fountain. A roundel barry-wavy argent and azure.

The aircraft of the Royal Air Force carry roundels of red, white and blue, the colours of the United Kingdom.

SEALS Seals have been in use for many centuries. They were used for 'signing' documents at a time when most people were unable to read or write. The use of heraldic seals began in England soon after the Norman Conquest. These seals bore the personal arms of the signatory (the person signing), which were engraved in reverse. When they were pressed on wax, the designs

came out the right way round. Seals were of gold, silver, brass, steel, or even lead. Some of them were very large. Signet rings were also used for sealing, and still are to-day. Supporters probably first came into being on seals (see SUPPORTERS).

Left: the seal of William de Wyndesore.

SEMÉ This term is used to describe a field strewn or scattered with small objects. It is then said to be semé of crescents', or whatever the objects may be. Here are some specialised terms relating to *semé:*

Not 'semé of cross-crosslets' but *crusilly*.

Not 'semé of fleurs-de-lis' but *semé-de-lis.*

Not 'semé of billets' but *billetty*.

Not 'semé of bezants' but *bezanty*.

Not 'semé of plates' but *platé.*

Not 'semé of gouttes' but *goutté* or *gutty* (see GOUTTE OR DROP).

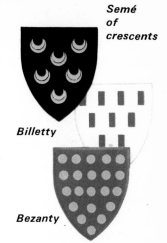

Semé of crescents

Billetty

Bezanty

SHIELD The shield is the most important part of the heraldic Achievement. Different names are given to different shapes of shield, such as Mantle, Buckler, Kite-shaped and Heater. The heraldic design of a shield consists of a background called the *Field* upon which objects may be placed (see FIELD). These are called *Charges* (see CHARGE). There are nine named points of the shield. By these one can show the exact position of a charge.

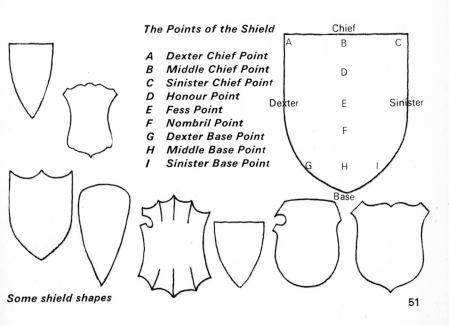

The Points of the Shield

A **Dexter Chief Point**
B **Middle Chief Point**
C **Sinister Chief Point**
D **Honour Point**
E **Fess Point**
F **Nombril Point**
G **Dexter Base Point**
H **Middle Base Point**
I **Sinister Base Point**

Chief

A B C
D
Dexter E Sinister
F
G H I

Base

Some shield shapes

Sometimes, shields bear above them certain types of head-gear. These indicate rank, as follows: for the monarch – A Closed Crown; for peers – Open Coronets; for Scots feudal barons – Chapeaux; for Bishops and Abbots – Mitres; for Scots Burghs – Mural Crowns; for Scottish County Councils – Wheatsheaf Coronets.

SINISTER Sinister means left-hand side. The sinister side of the shield is the left-hand side from the point of view of the man behind it. It is therefore on the right as seen by the viewer. (See also DEXTER.)

SUB-ORDINARIES These are charges almost as important as the Ordinaries, and frequently used. The main Sub-Ordinaries are:

Bordure. A border round the outside of the shield. It can be varied by using ornamental partition lines (see PARTITIONS OF THE SHIELD). In Scotland, the *bordure* is used for differencing (see CADENCY). It may be charged with other figures. Figures themselves may be placed in bordure. A bordure of lions is called 'a bordure of England'.

Orle. A narrow border set a little way in from the edge of the shield.

Double tressure. Two narrow Orles set close together. It is often 'flory counter flory', as in the arms of Scotland.

Inescutcheon. A small shield-shaped charge.

Quarter. A square figure occupying a quarter of the shield.

Canton. A small version of the Quarter. It is often used to carry augmentations. The Canton generally lies on top of everything else on the shield, obliterating what lies beneath it. (See AUGMENTATIONS AND ABATEMENTS OF HONOUR.)

Flanches. Large semi-circles, one on either side of the shield. They are never borne singly.

Some of the Sub-Ordinaries.

Bordure

Gyronny

Orle

Double tressure

Mascle

Gyron. A wedge-shaped piece stretching from the middle of the shield to the edge. If gyrons are repeated all round the field, it is said to be *gyronny,* and the number of pieces is usually stated. For instance: gyronny of twelve or and purpure'.

Lozenge. A diamond-shaped figure. When the entire field is covered with lozenges it is called *lozengy*. For instance 'lozengy or and vert' means covered with gold and green lozenges.

Fusil. Also diamond-shaped, but narrower than the lozenge.

Mascle. A 'voided' lozenge. This is a lozenge with a smaller lozenge removed from the centre.

Rustre. Lozenge with a round hole in the middle.

Roundel. A small circle (see ROUNDEL).

Annulet. A ring. It is the Mark of Cadency for a fifth son (see CADENCY).

Fret. A bendlet and a bendlet-sinister interlaced with a mascle (see ORDINARIES).

Fretty is the name for a field consisting of bendlets and bendlets-sinister interlaced all over the field.

Billet. An oblong figure set upright. A field scattered with billets is called *billetty.* If a billet is pointed at the base it is called *urdy at the foot.*

Chaplet. A garland of leaves, or leaves and flowers.

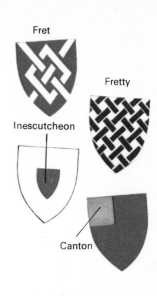

Fret

Fretty

Inescutcheon

Canton

Sable platy, two flanches argent

The Spelman Arms

Billet

Annulet

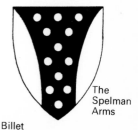

Quarterly of gules and ermine

Chaplet

ustre

Lozenge

Fusilly

SUPPORTERS The two figures which stand, one on either side of a shield, supporting it, are called supporters. They usually stand on a small grassy mound which is called a *compartment.* Supporters probably began on seals. When a shield of arms was placed in the middle of the seal, an empty space was left on either side, because of the rounded shape of the seal. Artists began to fill these spaces with imaginative animal figures. From this, the use of supporters for the shield developed.

Nowadays the use of Supporters is kept to Peers of the Realm; Knights of certain Orders; County, City and Borough Councils, and certain Corporations. Supporters may be humans, animals, monsters, birds, reptiles or fishes. They do not both have to be of the same kind. The Royal Arms have the Lion on one side and the Unicorn on the other, hence the nursery rhyme 'The Lion and the Unicorn were fighting for the crown'. There is a great variety of Supporters. The Corporation of Penzance has two pirates with cutlasses. Lord Rowallan has a salmon and a seal. Lord Brabazon of Tara has two seagulls carrying the armorial bearings aloft. Viscount Cowdray has a diver and a Mexican peon. Viscount Colville has a rhinoceros and Hercules.

TABARD A Tabard is a kind of surcoat, split down the sides with loose sleeves and held together by ties. It was used as a display for armorial bearings, and these were embroidered on it in gorgeous colours. They were worn by Heralds in olden times. Today they are worn on ceremonial occasions by Officers of the College of Heralds (see LIVERY).

A Talbot.

TALBOT The Talbot was the original heraldic dog, the hound of early days. The Talbot is still used a great deal as an inn-sign. It is often used as a Supporter (see SUPPORTERS).

THISTLE The Thistle is the floral emblem, or badge, of Scotland. It was the badge of James I of England and VI of Scotland. The Order of the Thistle is one of the highest of the Orders of Chivalry. The motto of the order is *nemo me impune lacessit* which means 'no one provokes me with impunity'.

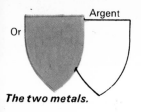

The two metals.

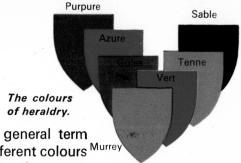

The colours of heraldry.

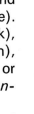

Murrey

A colour charge may NOT be placed upon a colour field.

TINCTURES This is a general term which refers to all the different colours and fabrics in which coats of arms are painted. There are two furs, two metals and eight colours. (For the two furs and their variants, see FURS.)

The two metals are *Or* (gold) and *Argent* (silver, or more usually, white).

The eight colours are *sable* (black), *azure* (blue), *gules* (red), *vert* (green), *purpure* (purple), *tenné* (orange or tawny), *murrey* (mulberry) and *sanguine* (blood red).

There are exact rules for the use of the tinctures. A metal charge may not be placed upon a metal field. A colour charge may not be placed upon a colour field. For instance, it is not possible to have a dolphin vert (green) on a field azure (blue). It is not permitted to have a chevron argent (silver) on a field or (gold).

However, colours may be placed upon metals or furs. Metals may be placed upon colours or furs. Furs may be placed upon colours or metals. The dolphin vert could be placed on a field or. It could also be placed on a field of argent, vair or ermine. The chevron argent could be placed on a field of any of the colours or furs.

In addition to the heraldic tinctures mentioned above, an object may be shown in its natural colouring. It is then described as *proper* and may be placed upon colours, or metals or furs, no matter what its own colouring may be (see PROPER).

TORSE OR WREATH The torse was a twist of material which bound the mantling to the helmet. In coats of arms it is shown as a twist of silk with a cord of metal twined round it. It rests on top of the helm, and supports the crest above. It must consist of six twists. The first is usually a metal but the other five may be of metals and colours.

A trick of the arms of the Heraldry Society
which are shown on the cover of this book.

TRICK To 'trick' means to indicate the tinctures of a coat of arms without using colour. The coat is sketched in black-and-white and the colours are shown in writing.

WOMEN'S ARMS *An unmarried lady* bears her father's arms on a lozenge, without Crest or Accessories (see SUB-ORDINARIES).

A married lady, if she is not heiress to her father's arms, will impale them with those of her husband on her husband's shield (see IMPALE). If she is heiress to her father's arms, they will be carried on an *Escutcheon of Pretence* in the middle of her husband's shield (see INESCUTCHEON). A married lady may *not* use her maiden arms by themselves. They must always be carried with those of her husband.

A widow combines the arms of her dead husband and herself on a lozenge, without Helm or Crest.

Peeresses. A peeress in her own right bears her inherited arms on a lozenge, with coronet and supporters, but without Helm or Crest.

Married peeresses. A peeress in her own right, when she marries, is allowed to carry her own arms on a lozenge. Her husband's arms, on his shield, are borne alongside. The two bearings form one Achievement, with Supporters, Coronets, and the husband's crest.

56

The College of Arms ●

In England, all heraldic matters are dealt with by the officers of the College of Arms. The College of Arms, or Heralds' College, is in London. The officers of the College have the following titles :

Kings of Arms
Garter King of Arms. He presides over the College.
Clarenceux King of Arms. He deals with heraldic matters south of the River Trent.
Norray and Ulster King of Arms. He deals with heraldic matters north of the River Trent.

Heralds of Arms
These are *Chester Herald, Lancaster Herald, Richmond Herald, Somerset Herald, Windsor Herald* and *York Herald.*

Pursuivants of Arms
These are called *Bluemantle, Portcullis, Rouge Croix* (Red Cross) and *Rouge Dragon* (Red Dragon).
The Earl Marshall (the Duke of Norfolk) has legal responsibility for the English Officers of Arms although he does not belong to the College of Arms. He arranges the ceremonies on State Occasions at which the Heralds have an important role.

The Court of the Lord Lyon ●

In Scotland, all heraldic matters are dealt with by the Lyon Court, which is in Edinburgh. The Officers have the following titles :

King of Arms
Lord Lyon King of Arms. He has full legal powers over all heraldic affairs in Scotland.

Heralds of Arms
These are *Marchmont Herald, Rothesay Herald* and *Albany Herald.*

Pursuivants of Arms
These are called *Dingwall, Unicorn* and *Carrick.*

● Arms of Different Kinds

Royal Arms

In a monarchy, the sovereign bears the arms of his country as his own. In the United Kingdom the reigning monarch is a direct descendant of the ancient sovereigns of England, Ireland, and Scotland. Therefore the hereditary arms of these kingdoms are born as his personal arms. Quartered in these arms are the golden lions of England, the red Lion of Scotland and the silver-and-gold Harp of Ireland.

Arms of other Nations

National flags are really Flags of Arms. They are used by people to show loyalty to their country.

Republics, such as Austria and Switzerland, have their own arms. The ancient republic of Florence had hers in very early times.

Most of the countries of the Commonwealth have their own arms, apart from their national flag.

Personal Arms

These are the arms which belong to a person or family. Nowadays, some people use them on signet rings and seals. They can also be engraved on cutlery, salvers, ashtrays or glassware, or printed on an heraldic bookplate.

Town and District Arms

These often contain some reference to the history of the district. They can often be seen on public buildings and monuments.

Corporate and Scholastic Arms

These include such arms as those of Abbeys, Banks, boards, clubs, fire-brigades, hospitals, ambulance-services, schools, masonic lodges and Universities. Some of the arms belonging to schools and Universities are very old indeed.

Ecclesiastical Arms

Church, or Ecclesiastical (eck-lees-ee-ass-tick-al) Arms are those of the Provinces and Sees (districts) of Archbishops and Bishops, religious houses and institutions.

Tracing Your Ancestry ●

In England, you may bear the arms of your ancestors on certain conditions. The arms must be officially recorded at the College of Arms. Also, you have to be able to prove that you are descended in the male line from the last bearer of the arms. If your descent is through a younger son, then you must 'difference' them.

If you have no hereditary right to bear arms, but wish to do so, you may apply to the College of Arms for arms of your own. If the applicant has a criminal record, or any other kind of discredit attaching to him, the request will not be granted. If the application is granted you pay a fee to have a new Patent of Arms prepared and painted. You and your descendants will then be entitled to bear those arms for ever.

In Scotland, you may bear arms yourself if you can prove that you are descended in the senior male line from someone who bore those arms. The arms must be registered in the Lyon Register. If you are descended through a younger son you must apply to the Lord Lyon for a suitable 'difference'.

If you cannot prove an hereditary right to Scottish arms, you may apply to Lord Lyon King of Arms for a special Grant of your own. If this is allowed it will entitle you and your descendants to arms. In Scotland, arms are protected by the full force of the law. Anyone who falsely uses your arms can be prosecuted and fined by Lyon Court.

The College of Arms can probably help you to trace your ancestry if you have an armorial bearing from which to start.

If you have no heraldic clues, the best place to begin is the General Register at Somerset House in London, where you may search the register indexes. If you trace your grandfather, you can get a copy of his birth certificate. This will tell you where he was born, and the names of his father and mother. You can then proceed to trace your great-grandfather and so on. The records at Somerset House only go back as far as 1837. If you wish to trace further back than that, you will have to consult such things as Census returns, Wills, parish registers etc.

● Index

Made and printed in Great Britain by Tinling (1973) Ltd.,
Prescot, Lancs. (a member of the Oxley Printing Group).

GEORGE V [George Frederick Ernest Albert]. Born 3 June 1865. Created Duke of York 1892, Prince of Wales 1901 and succeeded his father 6 May 1910. Died 20 January 1936.

=

Mary [Victoria Mary Augusta Louise Olga Pauline Claudine Agnes], daughter of Francis, Duke of Teck. Born 26 May 1867; married 6 July 1893 and died 24th March 1953.

EDWARD VIII [Edward Albert Christian George Andrew Patrick David. Born 23 June 1894. Created Prince of Wales 1910 & succeeded his father 20 Jan. 1936. Abdicated 10 Dec. 1936. Created Duke of Windsor 1937. Married 3rd June 1937 Bessie Wallis, daughter of Teakle Wallis Warfield and formerly wife of [1] Lieut. Spencer, U.S. Navy, and [2] Ernest Simpson.

GEORGE VI [Albert Frederick Arthur George]. Born 14 Dec. 1895. Created Duke of York 1920 and succeeded his brother 10 Dec. 1936. Died 6 Feb. 1952. Married 26 April 1923 Elizabeth [Angela Marguerite], daughter of Claude [Bowes-Lyon], Earl of Strathmore and Kinghorne.

ELIZABETH II [Elizabeth Alexandra Mary]. Born 21 April 1926. Married 20 Nov. 1947. Succeeded her father 22 June 1952.

=

Philip, Prince of Greece and Denmark. Born 10 June 1921. Naturalized a British subject and took surname of Mountbatten 1947. Created Duke of Edinburgh 1947.

Charles [Philip Arthur George]. Born 14 Nov. 1948. Created Prince of Wales 1958.

Andrew [Albert Christian Edward]. Born 19 Feb. 1960.